IN THE NAME OF ALLAH, MOST GRACIOUS, MOST MERCIFUL

ISLAM & MUSLIMS

Twenty-Five Questions & Answers

by
Dr. Ibrahim Abdul-Malik

SECOND PRINTING

"O mankind! We created you from a
single pair of a male and a female,
and made you into nations and tribes that
you might get to know one another,
(not that ye may despise each other).
Surely the noblest of you
in the sight of Allah is
he who is the most righteous."

(Malik, *Al-Hujurat, 49:13*)

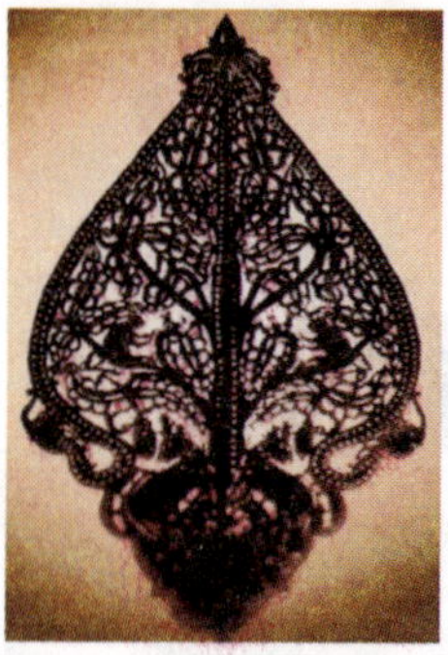

Booklet # 1 in Series

by

Dr. Ibrahim Abdul-Malik

Email: iam2379@yahoo.com

Dedicated to

People of Good Will everywhere, and to all Earnest Seekers who genuinely desire to learn more about Islam and Muslims.

The Qur'anic quotes throughout the document are taken ***mostly*** from:

The Meaning of THE HOLY QUR'AN, by Abdullah Yusuf **ALI** [*identified in text as* "**ALI**"]

Other quotations come from

The Message of THE QUR'AN by Muhammad **ASAD** [*identified in text as* "**ASAD**."]

THE ALIM, by ISL Software Corporation, translations by Muhammad M. **PICKTHALL** [*identified in text as* "**PICKTHALL**,"] and F. **MALIK** [*identified in text as* "**MALIK**."]

The Holy Qur'an by Amatul Rahman **OMAR** & Abdul Mannan **OMAR** [*identified in text as* "**OMAR & OMAR**."]

INTRODUCTION

I wrote this booklet in the atmosphere of fear and confusion that followed the devastating events of September 11, 2001.

Religious leaders everywhere constantly remarked on how Americans were flocking to churches, synagogues and masjids. We were all looking for answers. And in the process, we reached out to one another in ways that we had not done before.

As a Muslim, I was constantly plied with questions about Islam. "What do Muslims believe?" "Is this a holy war?" "Is Islam really a religion of violence?" And often, as I was being questioned, I imagined that my questioners were seeking more than information. I sensed that many of them were really looking for reassurances that their worst fears about Islam were not true. The booklet provided some answers, and allayed some fears.

It is now six years later. The pressure to learn more about our Muslim neighbors has eased. And yet the need for information about Islam seems as great as ever. ***The fact is that I still get many requests for copies of the booklet***. I am constantly pressed to explain (some even demand that I "justify") one or another thing about Islam. Regularly, I still hear disturbing misconceptions and half-truths about Islam sometimes even from persons who I thought knew better.

In response to the continuing demand for copies of the booklet, I offer this second printing. With this printing, I include a glossary of terms, a suggested list of titles for those readers who are interested in going further, and some words about the author.

I thank ALLAH for allowing me the opportunity to make this small contribution. I pray that it continues to clarify (where there is confusion), and enlighten (where there is ignorance). I pray that ALLAH continue to bless this effort. I pray that HE forgive my shortcomings; for ALLAH's message is perfect. Any imperfections are only mine, and mine alone.

i.a.m.

Wednesday, April 25, 2007

THE QUESTIONS

1. WHAT IS THE RELIGION OF ISLAM?
2. HOW DID THE RELIGION GET THE NAME "ISLAM"?
3. WHAT IS THE MEANING OF THE WORD "ISLAM"?
4. WHAT ARE THE WORDS OF THE MUSLIM GREETING? WHAT DO THEY MEAN?
5. WHO IS ALLAH?
6. WHAT IS THE DIFFERENCE BETWEEN "ISLAM" AND "MUSLIM"?
7. WHO ARE THE MUSLIMS?
8. WHAT DO MUSLIMS BELIEVE?
9. HOW DOES A PERSON BECOME A MUSLIM?
10. WHO IS MUHAMMAD?
11. HOW DID MUHAMMAD BECOME A PROPHET?
12. WHAT IS THE QUR'AN?
13. WHY IS THE QUR'AN IN ARABIC?

14. WHAT IS "HADEETH"?

15. WHAT ARE THE FIVE "PILLARS OF ISLAM"?

16. HOW DOES ISLAM REGARD JESUS AND MARY?

17. WHAT IS THE POSITION OF WOMEN IN ISLAM?

18. HOW IS ISLAM RELATED TO CHRISTIANITY AND JUDAISM?

19. WHO ARE "THE PEOPLE OF THE BOOK"?

20. WHAT DO MUSLIMS MEAN WHEN THEY SAY: "MAKE DU'A FOR ME"?

21. WHY DO MUSLIMS WORSHIP ON FRIDAYS, RATHER THAN ON SUNDAYS?

22. WHAT IS AN IMAM? HOW IS HE LIKE A PRIEST? A RABBI?

23. WHAT IS THE *REAL* MEANING OF "JIHAD"?

24. WHO ARE THE SUNNIS? HOW ARE THEY DIFFERENT FROM THE SHI'AHS?

25. WHAT DOES ISLAM SAY ABOUT THE TAKING OF INNOCENT LIVES? ABOUT TAKING ONE's OWN LIFE?

THE ANSWERS

1. WHAT IS ISLAM?

Islam is ***both*** a religion ***and*** a complete way of life. Islam is the religion and the way of life for more than a billion people throughout the world.

2. HOW DID THE RELIGION GET THE NAME "ISLAM"?

The names "Islam" and "Muslims" come from ALLAH, HIMSELF, who declared in the Qur'an:

> **"This day have I perfected your religion for you, completed my favor upon you, and *have chosen for you Islam* as your religion."** (Ali, *Al-Maida, 5:3*)
>
> ". . . *It is He Who has named you* **Muslims** both before, and in this (Revelation)." (Ali, *Al-Hajj, 22:78*)

3. WHAT IS THE MEANING OF THE WORD "ISLAM"?

The word "Islam" means **"submission,"** submission to the Will of ALLAH. The word "Islam" comes from the same root as the word "salaam," which means **"peace."** Through this submission, one finds ***internal*** peace.

> **". . . it is in the remembrance of Allah alone that the hearts really find peace."** (Omar & Omar, *Ar-Ra'd, 13:28*)

4. WHAT ARE THE WORDS OF THE MUSLIM GREETING? WHAT DO THEY MEAN?

The words of the Muslim greeting are: ***"As-salaamu alaikum,"*** and the response is ***"wa alaikum as-***

salaam." The greeting means: ***"Peace be with you."*** The response: ***"And with you, peace."***

5. WHO IS ALLAH?

The word "ALLAH" is the Arabic name for GOD - THE ONE, THE ONLY, THE UNIQUE, CREATOR OF THE UNIVERSE, and of everything that is in it. HE[1] is the very GOD of Christianity and Judaism. Like Arab Muslims, ***Arab Christians also address GOD as "ALLAH."*** The name "ALLAH" is used to refer ***only*** to the ONE GOD. The word "ALLAH," means "The God." The word "ALLAH" has no plural form.

6. WHAT IS THE DIFFERENCE BETWEEN "ISLAM" AND "MUSLIM"?

"Islam" is the name of the religion. Persons who practice Islam are called **"Muslims."**

7. WHO ARE THE MUSLIMS?

They represent virtually every race, nationality, ethnic group and culture on the face of the globe. They add up to more than one billion people. ***Only about 18% of Muslims in the world are Arabs***.

The world's most populous ***Muslim*** country is Indonesia. India, Pakistan and Bangladesh are home to many millions of Muslims. Most of the African continent is Muslim, and substantial numbers of Muslims are found in Canada, USA, South American countries, in Europe, China, Russia and the surrounding countries. African Americans make up some **42%** of American Muslims.

8. WHAT DO MUSLIMS BELIEVE?

The *Six* Articles of Muslim Faith are:

I. **ACCEPTANCE of**, and **FAITH in ALLAH alone**, as THE ONE GOD, THE ONE and ONLY. HE has NO associates. HE does not beget, nor was HE HIMSELF begotten.

II. Belief in the **ANGELS OF ALLAH.**

III. Belief in the **BOOKS OF ALLAH.** These books are: the **Torah**, the **Psalms** of David, the **Gospel** of Jesus, and the Qur'an. (**Ali, *Al-i'lmran, 3:3***)

IV. Belief in the **MESSENGERS OF ALLAH**. Some of these messengers were **Noah, Abraham, Moses, Jesus**, and **Muhammad** (*pbut*)[2].

According to the Qur'an, Muhammad is *"the Seal of the Prophets,"* (**Ali, *Al-Ahzab, 33:40***), *i.e.*, he is the ***final*** link in the long chain of Messengers whom **ALLAH** has sent to humankind.

V. Belief in **THE LAST DAY** – the **DAY OF JUDGMENT**, and in the **HEREAFTER.**

VI. Belief in **DIVINE ORDINANCE**. ALLAH'S laws operate in every phase of our lives. When we obey those laws, we are rewarded. When we violate them, we suffer the consequences.

9. HOW DOES A PERSON BECOME A MUSLIM?

A person becomes a Muslim by making a sincere, ***public*** declaration of faith before witnesses. The words of the declaration are: *"laa ilaaha illa llah, muhammadun rasulu llah,"* (There is no god but ALLAH, [and] Muhammad is a messenger of ALLAH).

10. WHO IS MUHAMMAD?

Muhammad was the person to whom ALLAH sent the Angel Gabriel to reveal the Qur'an – the Holy Book of Islam. The revelations began when Muhammad was 40 years old, and lasted until his death, 23 years later.

Muhammad was an Arab who lived in Mecca, which is today part of Saudi Arabia. He belonged to the influential tribe of Quraish. His father died before he was born, and his mother died when he was six years old. He was raised by his uncle, his father's brother.

As a young man, Muhammad was very contemplative. He would frequently spend many hours, sometimes many days, meditating in his favorite mountain cave outside the city limits.

Early in his life he established a reputation for being honest and dependable. In fact, he was known by the nickname "Al-Amin" – the trustworthy one.

Muhammad married Khadija, a wealthy widow, when he was 25 years old, and she was 40. They had six children, two boys and four girls. Both boys died in infancy.

Fifteen years into the marriage, Muhammad began receiving the revelations during one of his meditative sessions in the cave. He was so overwhelmed by this experience, that he rushed home to his wife, looking for comfort and reassurance.

In this instance, as in so many others in later years, she proved to be his staunchest supporter. Indeed, Khadija was the **first person to accept the message** that Muhammad brought through the revelations he received.

Their marriage lasted 25 years, ending only when she died at age 65. **For the full duration of their marriage, Khadija was the Prophet's only wife.**

Following Khadija's death, Prophet Muhammad married first a widow to take care of his household, and then at different times, several other wives.

But life for Muhammad was not always benign. For years, he and the early Muslims were the targets and victims of severe persecution from powerful enemies - many of them from his own tribe.

Life eventually became so unbearable for them, that they secretly fled their homes in Mecca for the more welcoming environment of Medina, a city 260 miles north of Mecca.

This ***"hijra,"*** as it is known in Arabic (the word means "flight") was a mutually satisfying arrangement. Warring tribes in Medina were wreaking havoc throughout the city, and matters were really getting out of hand.

Prophet Muhammad was invited to help bring peace to the city. And of course, this meant that the Prophet and his Muslim community would find refuge from the atrocities they had been suffering in Mecca at the hands of their persecutors.

During the next ten years, Muhammad achieved many successes. A prophet, Muhammad was also teacher and judge. In Medina, he proved himself to be the Statesman *extraordinaire*.

He created a model society in Medina, where Christians and Jews and the new Muslims, lived in harmony and mutual respect. Throughout the same period, the Prophet continued to receive divine revelations. Scholars agree that the last revelation was:

> **"And fear the day when [you] shall be brought back to Allah. Then shall every soul be paid what it earned, and none shall be dealt with unjustly."** (Ali, *Al-Baqara, 2:281*)

The Prophet died peacefully in his 63rd year.

11. HOW DID MUHAMMAD BECOME A PROPHET?

When the Angel Gabriel approached Muhammad with the first revelation from ALLAH, and repeatedly commanded him to ***"READ! in the name of thy Lord . . ."*** (Ali, *Al-Alaq, 96:1*). Muhammad had clearly been selected by ALLAH to be HIS prophet. And indeed, the continuing revelations over the next 23 years confirm it.

12. WHAT IS THE QUR'AN?

The Qur'an is for Muslims what The Bible is for Christians, or The Torah for Jews. The Qur'an, divine in origin, is the ***primary*** source of authoritative instructions for Muslim living.

The Qur'an was revealed over a period of 23 years to Prophet Muhammad, in the Arabic language. If there were any doubt that these revelations were from ALLAH, hear the words of confirmation:

> **"Thus have WE sent, by inspiration, to [you] an Arabic Qur'an."** (Ali, *Ash-Shura, 42:7*)
>
> **"Verily, WE have revealed The Book to [you], in truth, for instructing mankind."** (Ali, *Az-Zumar, 39:41*)
>
> **"And if you doubt any part of what WE have bestowed from on high, step by step, upon our servant (Muhammad), then produce a surah of similar merit. . . ."** (Asad, *Al-Baqara, 2:23*)[3]

With each revelation, the words were impressed upon the heart of Prophet Muhammad. After each revelation, he taught the words to his companions.

During this period, scribes also wrote down the words. By the time of the Prophet's death, many persons had memorized the entire Qur'an, and often recited it *in part* or *in whole*.

That practice of memorizing and reciting is entirely consistent with two relevant facts:

i. This society had a strong ***oral*** tradition. That is, they depended on their memories, the way we depend on the written word.

ii. The word "Qur'an" means "recite," "recitation."

The tradition of reciting the Qur'an is as alive today, more than1400 years later, as it was in the Prophet's time. And the words being recited are precisely the words that Muhammad and his Companions recited.

Indeed, within twenty years of Muhammad's death, the entire Qur'an had been set down in the standardized, written form we know today. The purpose for so doing was to ensure accuracy in the reading and reciting of The Book, especially by Muslims whose first language was not Arabic.

As this work was being carried out, there was the constant collaboration between the scribes and the memorizers – the two groups serving as a kind of "checks and balances" on each other. The net effect of this interaction was to virtually guarantee the accuracy of the written product.[4] Significant, too, with respect to the purity of the Qur'an, is the promise of ALLAH:

> **"WE have without doubt sent down The Message, and *WE will assuredly guard it from corruption*." (Ali, *Al-Hijr, 15:9*)**

Qur'an, a single book of 114 chapters, refers to itself by many names: *"A Guide to Mankind"; "A Book Full of Blessings"; "A Book That Makes Things Clear"; "Glad Tidings to Those Who Do Right"; "The Book Explaining All Things"; "A Healing"; "A Well-Guarded Book"; "The Revelation of ALLAH"; "The Truth."*

13. WHY IS THE QUR'AN IN ARABIC?

The Qur'an itself gives the answer:

"We have made this Qur'an easy *in your own language*, so that you may give good news to the righteous, and warn the headstrong, contentious folk." (Malik, *Maryam*, 19:97)

"We have revealed this Qur'an in the Arabic language, so that you (Arabs) may understand." (Malik, *Yusuf*, 12:2)

Remember that Prophet Muhammad who received the revelations was Arabic-speaking, as were his people. For this reason, any translation of the Qur'an, is NOT ***The*** Qur'an, but "The Message of the Qur'an," or "The Meaning of the Qur'an." ***The*** Qur'an is only the actual words of the revelation, and those words are in Arabic.

14. WHAT IS "HADEETH"?

In question 12 above, you read the sentence: "The Qur'an is the ***primary*** source of authoritative instructions for Muslim living."

You may well have wondered at that time: Is there a ***secondary*** source? and if so, What is it? The answers are ***"yes,*** there is a secondary source of authoritative instructions for Muslim living," ***and*** "the name of that source is ***'the hadeeth.' "*** Unlike Qur'an, hadeeth are of human origin.

"Hadeeth" is the Arabic word for ***the authenticated, collected traditions that are based on the reported speech, thoughts and actions of Prophet Muhammad.*** These traditions, also called ***"The Sunnah,"*** are second in importance only to The Qur'an.

15. WHAT ARE THE FIVE "PILLARS OF ISLAM"?

In the same way that a pillar is a support structure for a building, so are certain religious practices the support structures of our Muslim faith. Five such "support structures" exist in Islam, and are popularly known as the "PILLARS OF ISLAM." They are:

I. **THE SHAHAADAH** – the ***public*** **declaration of faith**. The words are: ***"laa ilaaha illa llah, muhammadun rasulu llah,"*** and the meaning: "There is no god but ALLAH, [and] Muhammad is a Messenger of ALLAH."

II. **SALAAH – obligatory, *formal* prayers**. These are performed *five* times daily. These obligatory, ***formal*** prayers are perhaps the most widely recognized activity of Islam. They may be performed in groups or alone, in the Mosque or in any other location. They are said at ***dawn***, at ***noon***, in the ***afternoon***, in the ***evening***, and at ***night***. [See answer to question 20]

III. **ZAKAAT – obligatory tax.** This tax is to be used for charity. Qur'an calls Zakaat "a Loan to ALLAH," who has promised: ***"Spend on charity, and I will spend on you."*** (*Hadeeth Qudsi, 11*).

IV. **SAWM – fasting during the month of Ramadan**. Fasting is obligatory on all Muslims who are physically able to endure the challenges of the practice.

V. **THE HAJJ – pilgrimage to Mecca.** This pilgrimage is obligatory (at least *once* in a lifetime) on every sane Muslim who is *physically* and *financially* able to make the journey. Every year, millions of Muslims from around the globe converge on Mecca, the Holy City in Saudi Arabia, in which is located Islam's holiest shrine – the **Kaabah**. According to Qur'an, this cube-shaped structure was built by Abraham and his son Ishmael. (*Al-Baqara, 2:125, 127*)

When Muslims say their formal prayers, they turn in the direction of the Kaabah, which is also called "the House of ALLAH." A highlight of the pilgrimage is the circling of the Kaabah by the faithful.

16. HOW DOES ISLAM REGARD JESUS AND MARY?

The Qur'an instructs us to honor ***all*** of ALLAH's Prophets and Messengers, those named, and those unnamed. We are also reminded to make no differences ***"between one and another among them."*** (**Ali,** ***Al-i 'Imran, 3:84***)

Jesus was one of ALLAH's greatest Messengers, born miraculously of a ***virgin*** mother. As Qur'an records:

> **[The angel said]: ". . . I am only a messenger from thy Lord, (to announce) to thee the gift of a holy son. . . . as a Sign unto men, and a Mercy from Us. It is a matter (so) decreed. So she conceived him, and she retired with him to a remote place." (Ali, *Maryam, 19:19-22*)**

> **"Verily, in the sight of GOD, the nature of Jesus is as the nature of Adam, whom HE created out of dust, and then said unto HIM: 'Be' – and he is." (Asad, *Al-ilmran, 3:59*)**

> **"To Jesus the son of Mary, WE gave clear (Signs), and strengthened him with the Holy Spirit."** (Ali, *Al-Baqara, 2:253*)[3]

> **". . . his name will be Christ Jesus, the son of Mary, held in honor in this world and the Hereafter, and of (the company of) *those nearest to Allah*."** (Ali, *Al-i 'Imran, 3:45*)

Jesus is therefore held in very high regard, as is his mother, Mary, for whom a chapter in the Qur'an is named. Listen to the words of Qur'an:

> **"O Mary! Allah hath chosen [you], and purified [you]; *chosen [you] above the women of all nations*."** (Ali, *Al-i 'Imran, 3:42*)

> **"And (remember) her who guarded her chastity. *We breathed into her of Our Spirit*, and *We made her and her son a Sign for all peoples*."** (Ali, *Al-Anbiyaa, 21:91*)

To honor a Prophet, however, does ***not*** mean to worship him/her. Muslims worship ***only*** ALLAH. Accordingly, in Islam, Jesus, Muhammad and all of the other Prophets of ALLAH are only human beings, however great their contributions.

> **"O people of the Book! Commit no excesses in your religion, nor say of Allah aught but truth. *Christ Jesus the son of Mary was (no more than) an Apostle of Allah*. . . ."** (Ali, *An-Nisaa, 4:171*)

> **"It is not conceivable that GOD should have taken unto HIMSELF a son. Limitless is HE in HIS glory. When HE wills a thing to be, HE but says unto it: " 'Be'! And it is."** (Asad, *Maryam, 19:35*)

17. WHAT IS THE POSITION OF WOMEN IN ISLAM?

Entire books have been written on this topic. It follows, then, that any answer given here must necessarily be incomplete, barely scratching the surface. We will address only *three* aspects of the question:

A. Do women in Islam have gender equity with men?

B. Does Islam require women to wear the head coverings?

C. How is it that Muslim men can have more than one wife?

A. Before Islam came to the seventh century Arabs, they were a loosely organized society of tribes who were constantly warring with each other.

Most women in this pre-Islamic society, known as the age of ignorance (*jahiliiya),* were truly second-class citizens. They were completely dominated by men, and had no opportunities to reverse these oppressive conditions.

Typical of their status was the fact that they were prevented from inheriting property. When a parent (*i.e.* a father) died, his property was divided among his sons. His daughters got nothing.

Actually, it was worse than that. For example, a son could inherit his father's wife (assuming, of course, she was not his mother). Children, too, (***both male and female***) were often also excluded from their "rightful" inheritances.

Then along came Prophet Muhammad and his revelations, bringing a message of ***"equality and dignity for all, for men and women, [for] masters and servants."***[5]

In its own words, the Qur'an makes the case:

> **"O [you] who believe, *[you] are forbidden to inherit women against their will*. Nor should [you] treat them with harshness, that [you] may take away part of the dower [which you] have given them, except where they have been guilty of open lewdness. On the contrary, live with them on *a footing of kindness and equity*."** (**Ali**, *An-Nisaa, 4:19*)

> **"For Muslim men and *women*, for believing men and *women*, for devout men and *women*, for true men and *women*, for men and *women* who are patient and constant, for men and *women* who humble themselves, for men and *women* who give in charity, for men and *women* who fast (and deny themselves), for men and *women* who guard their chastity, and for men and *women* who engage much in Allah's praise, for them has Allah prepared forgiveness and great reward."** (**Ali**, *Al-Ahzab, 33:35*)

> **"*Men* shall have a share in what parents and kinsfolk leave behind, and *women* shall have a share in what parents and kinsfolk leave behind, whether it be little or much - a share ordained [by God]."** (**Asad**, *An-Nisaa, 4:7*)

"<u>*Men*</u> shall have a benefit from what they earn, <u>and *women*</u> shall have a benefit from what they earn." (Asad, *An-Nisaa, 4:32*)

"Whereas any one, <u>*be it man or woman*</u>, who does [whatever he can] of good deeds, and is a believer withal, shall enter paradise." (Asad, *An-Nisaa, 4:124*) [see also *Al-i 'Imran, 3:195*]

"The believers, <u>*men and women*</u>, are protectors one of another." (Ali, *At-Tauba, 9:71*)

The Qur'an could not be clearer about its position on gender equity between men and women. It is not too much to suggest that these Qur'anic declarations were revolutionary, given the traditional status of women in pre-Islamic times. It is also not too much to suggest that many men would have been very unhappy with these new developments – and for quite understandable reasons.

In very practical terms, these new requirements meant that men would get a smaller share of the available wealth than they were used to.

But more disturbing for some of them, perhaps, would be the cessation of their male privileges, and the disruption of the patterns they had practiced for generations. Suddenly, women were put on an equal footing with them, and this was a challenge, to say the least.

We have seen how, repeatedly, when the Qur'an issues a statement about men, immediately in the same verse or in the next, Qur'an repeats the statement for women. Women had gained a dignity that matched their new status, and that status and dignity are still in force. Qur'an's ***position on women has <u>not</u> changed***.

Today, it is still true that **<u>Islam</u>** regards a woman, whether single or married, as an individual in her own right. She has every right to her own property and earnings, and may dispose of them as she sees fit.

When she marries, she may keep her own family name, rather than adopt that of her husband. The marital gift presented to her by her husband is for her own personal use, hers to share (or not to share) with husband and/or family, *only as she chooses*.

Qur'an so honors women, that it issues very strict penalties for any one who falsely accuses a woman of being "unchaste."

> **"And as for those who accuse chaste women [of adultery], and then are unable to produce four witnesses [in support of their accusation], flog them with eighty stripes, and ever after, refuse to accept from them any testimony, since it is they - they [who] are truly depraved."** (**Asad, *An-Nur, 24:4***)

As equal partners in Islam, women and men play ***complementary*** roles, each vitally important to the family. Islam accords the highest esteem to ***mothers.***[7] Clearly, the needs of the family are best served when father and mother have a ***collaborative*** attitude towards each other. It is against the guidance of Qur'an, when either husband or wife oppresses the other. ***It is against the teachings of Islam when men oppress women.***

B. The question asks: ***Does Islam require women to wear the head coverings?*** Following are the instructions in the Qur'an:

> **"Tell the believing *men* to lower their gaze, and to be mindful of their chastity* . . .And tell the believing *women* to lower their gaze, and to be mindful of their chastity. . . ." (Asad, *An-Nur, 24:30-31*)**
>
> **". . . and not to display their charms [in public], beyond what may [decently] be apparent thereof. Hence, let them draw their head coverings** over their bosoms. And let them not**

---

*According to **Muhammad Asad**, in The Message of THE QUR'AN, (**note #36, p. 538**), the sentence: "lower their gaze, and be mindful of their modesty" could literally be translated: ***"to restrain something of their gaze, and to guard their private parts."***

He suggests a dual meaning for the second part of the literal translation: **1**. actually covering their private parts; *i.e.*, dress modestly, and **2**. controlling their sexual urges, by expressing them ***only*** with their spouses.

In (note #38, p. 538-539**), Asad writes: ". . . the head-covering [was] customarily used by Arabian women **before** and **after** the advent of Islam. According to most of the classical commentators, it was worn in pre-Islamic times more or less as an ornament, and was let down loosely over the wearer's back. And since, in accordance with the fashion of the time, the upper part of a woman's tunic had a wide opening in the front, her breasts were left bare. Hence the injunction to cover the bosom by means of a [head-covering]. . .

"[The injunction] **does not necessarily relate to the use of a [head-covering] as such**, but is rather meant to make it clear that a woman's breasts are not included in the concept of 'what may decently be apparent' of her body, and should not, therefore, be displayed."

display [more of] their charms to any but their husbands. ..." (Asad, *An-Nur, 24:31*)

"O Prophet, tell [your] wives and [your] daughters, as well as all [other] *believing women,* that they should draw over themselves some of their outer garments [when in public]. This will be more conducive to *their being recognized [as decent women]* and not annoyed. But . . . God is indeed much forgiving, a dispenser of Grace." (Asad, *Al-Ahzab, 33:59*)

The Qur'an requires both men and women to dress modestly. How that modesty is expressed is interpreted differently from one society to another, from one time to another.

Accordingly, many of the traditions of female attire reflect those cultural interpretations, as well as the customs of the particular area where they are found. In short, what is often "justified" as being "Islamic" is typically more rooted in cultural traditions and local customs, than in Qur'anic teachings.

In a similar way, the treatment which Muslim women in certain parts of the Muslim world receive at the hands of Muslim men almost always reflects cultural practices and preferences.

In too many instances, these practices and preferences are inconsistent with authentic Islamic teachings, even at times contradicting them outright.

C. In this section, we look at the question: ***How is it that Muslim men can have more than one wife***? In

Qur'an we read:

> **"... marry from among [other] women such as are lawful to you - [even] *two*, or *three*, or *four*. But if you have reason to fear that you might not be able to treat them with equal fairness, *then [only] one*...."** (**Asad, *An-Nisaa, 4:3***)
>
> **"And *it will not be within your power to treat your wives with equal fairness, however much you may desire it*. And so, do not allow yourselves to incline towards one, to the exclusion of the other, leaving her in a state, as it were, of having, and not having a husband. But if you put things to rights, and are conscious of Him - behold, GOD is indeed much-forgiving, a dispenser of grace."** (**Asad, *An-Nisaa, 4:129***)

The simple answer to the question is that Qur'an does give permission. But take note that it is ***permission with a condition***. And what is the condition? ***The man must treat all of his wives with "equal fairness."*** If he has reason to believe that he will not be able to do so, then he can have ***only one wife***.

And then there is the verse which states categorically that

> **"It *will not be* within your power to treat your wives with equal fairness, *however much you may desire it*."** (**Asad, *An-Nisaa, 4:129***)

This verse certainly seems to lessen the force of the permission. For if it is beyond the power of men to satisfy the stated condition for the permission, then isn't Islam advocating ***"one man, one wife"***?

Muhammad Asad agrees. In his (***note #147, p. 130***) he

writes: "In view of the fact that a man's behaviour towards another person is, in the long run, almost inevitably influenced by what he *feels* about that person, ***the above passage . . . imposes a moral restriction on plural marriages."***

18. HOW IS ISLAM RELATED TO CHRISTIANITY AND JUDAISM?

Islam, Christianity and Judaism are the three great monotheistic religions of the world. That is, these three religions teach that there is only ONE GOD.

These three religions spring from the same Patriarch, ***Abraham*** (in Islam, we call him ***"Ibrahim"***). In fact, they are often referred to as the ***"Abrahamic Religions."*** These three religions honor the same prophets and messengers who, throughout the ages, brought ALLAH's message to humankind.

The Qur'an teaches that the GOD of Islam is the same GOD to whom Christians pray, is the same GOD to whom Jews pray. In Islam we say "ALLAH." The Christians say "GOD." The Jews say "ADONAI." But we are all addressing the same CREATOR, the same GOD of love and forgiveness, the same GOD to whom we will all answer on the Day of Judgment.

> **"And dispute you not with the *People of the Book*, . . . but say: 'We [Muslims] believe in the Revelation which has come down to *us*, and in that which came down to *you*. *Our Allah and your Allah is one*; and it is to HIM we bow (in Islam)' "** (Ali, *Al-Ankabut, 29:46*)

19. WHO ARE THE "PEOPLE OF THE BOOK"?

The designation, "The People of the Book" refers to Muslims, Christians and Jews. One of GOD's Prophets, Moses (*Musa*), brought the ***Torah*** to the Jews. Another, Jesus (*Isa*), brought the ***Gospel*** to Christians. And still another, Muhammad, brought the Qur'an to Muslims, (*initially*, to Arabs, and *ultimately*, to all humankind).

Islam teaches that ALLAH's message has ***always*** been the same, whoever the Messenger delivering it, whoever the people to whom it was sent, whatever the period in human history.

> **"Surely, We have sent down (Our) revelation to you, as We sent it down to Noah, and the Prophets (who came) after him. And We sent revelation to Abraham, Ismail, Isaac, Jacob and his children, and to Jesus, Job, Jonah, Aaron and Solomon. And We gave David a Scripture."**
> **(Omar & Omar, *An-Nisaa, 4:163*)**

In time, for a variety of reasons, the message underwent changes - *omissions, errors, additions, distortions, losses*. It follows, then, that by the time of the revelations to Prophet Muhammad (pbuh), the surviving textual versions of the message must necessarily have been incomplete, ***at best***, and inaccurate in important places, ***at worst***.

Accordingly, the full message was again revealed to Prophet Muhammad, with the reassuring promise from ALLAH that this time, the message will be preserved without corruption.

"Behold, it is WE, OURSELVES, who have bestowed from on high, step by step, this reminder [Qur'an]. And behold, *it is WE who shall truly guard it [from all corruption]*." **(Asad, *Al-Hijr*, 15:9)**[3]

20. WHAT DO MUSLIMS MEAN WHEN THEY SAY: "MAKE DU'A FOR ME"?

They mean **"Pray for me."** The unfamiliar language simply reflects the fact that in Islam, prayers are both *formal* and *informal*.

You have already read about the *formal* prayers in the answer to question 15, (the second pillar). These ***formal*** prayers are called **"salaah,"** and Muslims are obligated to recite them, in Arabic, ***five*** times a day.

The ***informal*** prayers are called **"du'a."** They are not obligatory, and may be said at any time, as often as you feel, in whatever language you speak.

21. WHY DO MUSLIMS WORSHIP ON FRIDAYS, RATHER THAN ON SUNDAYS?

The authority for this practice comes from both the Qur'an and Prophet Muhammad, through authentic hadeeth.

From the Qur'an:

"O [you] who believe! when the call is proclaimed to prayer on Friday (the Day of Assembly), hasten earnestly to the Remembrance of Allah, and leave off business (and traffic). That is best for you, if [you] but knew!" (Ali, *Al-Jumu'a*, 62:9)

From authenticated hadeeth:

> **"For the Jews (the day set aside for prayer) was Sabt (Saturday), and for the Christians it was Sunday. And Allah turned towards us and guided us to Friday (as the day of prayer) for us. In fact, He (Allah) made Friday, Saturday and Sunday (as days of prayer)."[6]** (*Muslim, 417*)

22. WHAT IS AN IMAM? HOW IS HE LIKE A PRIEST? A RABBI?

Literally, the word "Imam" means "*he who stands in front of others,*" hence the person who leads a congregational or group prayer. In actual practice, an Imam is an Islamic religious leader. Generally, he is the leader of a congregation, although that is not a necessary condition for being an Imam.

Traditionally, the person selected ***by the community*** to be an Imam is considered to be the one ***among them*** who is most knowledgeable about the Qur'an and hadeeth.

> **"When there are three persons, one of them should lead . . . [the prayer]. The one among them most worthy to act as Imam is [the] one who is best versed in the Qur'an and Sunnah."** (*Muslim, 326 & 327*)

In this regard, the Imam is like the Priest, or the Rabbi. For by virtue of their training and knowledge, they are all qualified to lead their actual or potential congregations.

But there is an important difference. The Priest (in Christianity), and the Rabbi (in Judaism) are representatives of an ordered class (the ***Priesthood*** and the ***Rabbinate***) that is an integral part of the structure of these religions.

The Imams in Islam do not represent such an ordered class, for the simple reason that the concept of humans' conferring holy orders upon others does not exist in Islam.

What we do have are many highly respected Islamic scholars (*Ulamaa*). They represent the pinnacle of Islamic knowledge, practice and thought.

23. WHAT IS THE REAL MEANING OF "JIHAD"?

Judging from the seeming surety with which so many persons talk about "jihad" as a "holy war," waged by Muslims against the entire non-Muslim world, one might therefore wonder why this question? Isn't it true that "jihad" means "holy war"? The answer is "yes," and "no."

Yes, it is true that some translators render the word "jihad" as "holy war." But that is only the ***lesser*** part of the story. No, it is not true, if by "holy war" is meant that we Muslims have the right to declare war on whomever we choose, whenever we choose.

Let us now explore the meaning of the statement: *"Jihad is 'holy war'."* The Qur'an is very clear that Muslims have the right to ***defend*** themselves when attacked, to fight ***defensive*** wars to protect the Faith.

But we are warned not to be excessive in our response. And further, the moment the enemy stops fighting and seeks peace, we are instructed to end all hostilities. Hear the words of Qur'an:

> **"Fight, in the cause of Allah, those who fight you. *But do not transgress limits*; for Allah loveth not transgressors."** (**Ali, *Al-Baqara, 2:190***)

> **"To those against whom war is made, permission is given (to fight), because they are wronged. And verily, Allah is most powerful for their aid."** (**Ali, *Al-Hajj, 22:39***)

> **". . . but if they cease, *let there be no hostility*, except to those who practice oppression."** (**Ali, *Al-Baqara, 2:193***)

> **"But if the enemy incline towards peace, *do [you] (also) incline towards peace*, and trust in Allah; for HE is the one that heareth and knoweth [all things]."** (**Ali, *Al-Anfal, 8:61***)

The much more important meaning of the word "Jihad" is "*struggle,*" or "*striving.*" And indeed, this meaning represents the ***greater*** jihad. For the struggle is within oneself, and refers to the great effort it requires to "put God's will into practice at every level - personal and social, as well as political."[5]

This struggle is a constant in our daily living. Controlling one's anger, exercising the patience and perseverance to achieve those personal goals that foster righteous living, ***that is jihad***.

> **"The strong is not the one who overcomes the people by his strength, *but the strong is the one who controls himself while in anger*."** (***Al-Bukhari, vol. 8, #135***)

"Behold! As for those who attain to Faith, and do righteous deeds, We do not fail to requite any *who persevere in doing good*." (Asad, *Al-Kahf, 18:30*)

Finding and exercising the courage to speak truth to power, ***that is jihad***. Doing the difficult thing (***because it is morally right***), as opposed to taking the easy way that would violate your moral principles, ***that is jihad***. Working to relieve the suffering of victims of injustice, or to improve the living conditions in the society, ***that is jihad***.

It is these internal struggles to purify our souls, to ward off the ubiquitous invitations to do evil, to live each day more righteously than we did the day before, these are the elements that make up ***THE GREATER JIHAD***.

24. WHO ARE THE SUNNIS? HOW ARE THEY DIFFERENT FROM THE SHI'AHS?

Islam is divided into two major branches - the Sunnis and the Shi'ahs. The Sunnis, who make up the majority group, take their name from the *Sunnah* (traditions) of Prophet Muhammad (*pbuh*).[2] ***[see answer to question 14]***

The Shi'ahs believe that, Ali, the cousin and son-in-law of Prophet Muhammad, should have been his first successor as leader of the Muslims. The name "Shi'ah" means "party," hence the Shi'ahs are the Party of Ali, the Supporters of Ali.

But whether "Sunni" or "Shi'ah," we are all Muslims -

those who submit to the Will of ALLAH. And despite whatever differences, we pray in the same way, we honor Prophet Muhammad (*pbuh*), we live by the same articles of Faith, we revere ALLAH's message as it is written in the Holy Qur'an.

25. WHAT DOES ISLAM SAY ABOUT THE TAKING OF INNOCENT LIVES? ABOUT TAKING ONE'S OWN LIFE?

On this life and death question, Al-Qur'an and the Prophet have the definitive answer:

> **". . . If anyone slays a human being - unless it be [in punishment] for murder, or for spreading corruption on earth - it shall be as though he had slain all mankind. Whereas, if anyone saves a life, it shall be as though he had saved the lives of all mankind." . . (Asad, *Al-Maida, 5:32*) [see also: *Al-Israa, 17:33*]**

> **"But whoever deliberately slays a believer, his requital shall be hell, therein to abide. And GOD will condemn him, and will reject him, and will prepare for him awesome suffering." (Asad, *An-Nisaa, 4:93*)**

> **"Hence, do not kill your children for fear of poverty, . . . Verily, killing them is a great sin." (Asad, *Al-Israa, 17:31*)**

> **"Whoever commits suicide with something, will be punished with the same thing in the (Hell) fire." (*Al-Bukhari, vol. 8, #126*)**[6]

> **"The Prophet said, 'The biggest of (the great sins) are [four]: (1) to join others as partners in worship with Allah, (2) <u>to murder a human being,</u> . . .' " (*Al-Bukhari, vol. 9, #10*)**

"The Prophet said, 'The first cases to be decided among the people (on the Day of Resurrection) will be those of bloodshed.'" (*Al-Bukhari, vol. 9, #4*)

ISLAMIC ASTROLABE
(Syria, 628 C.E.)[7]

END NOTES

[1] The use of the masculine pronoun, HE, to refer to ALLAH, is in accordance with common *linguistic* usage, and is **not** intended to suggest that ALLAH has a gender. In fact, Qur'an rejects ascribing any human form to GOD. Instead, Qur'an helps us to "know" ALLAH through HIS many divine attributes, as expressed in the descriptive names by which HE is known – **the "Most Beautiful Names." Qur'an** encourages Muslims to use these names when they address the CREATOR.

[2] **"pbut"** is the acronym for the prayer: *Peace and Blessings be Upon **Them**.* When the prayer is for only one person, the acronym is: **"pbuh,"** *Peace and Blessings be Upon **Him/Her**.*

[3] **(Notice this use of the word "WE," the first person plural. Often in Qur'an when ALLAH speaks, HE uses "WE" to refer to HIMSELF).**

[4] Arabic is traditionally written **without** vowels. But in the standardized, written version of Qur'an, all vowels and other diacritical marks are inserted in the text.

This process of inserting these linguistic guides insures that wherever in the world the Qur'an is read, the renderings will be the same. Furthermore, the reciters, particularly the non-Arab ones, will have the proper written guidance with respect to the correct pronunciation of the words.

When we consider the fact that the overwhelming majority of Muslims in the world today are non-Arab, we can truly appreciate the wisdom of that early decision.

[5] **Karen Armstrong**, in "The True, Peaceful Face of Islam," in TIME, October 1, 2001, p. 48. You will notice her use of the word "equality," which, in the minds of many, implies a mathematical equivalency. I have chosen instead to use the word "equity," which carries the sense of fairness and justice in dealings.

[6] **Muslim** and **Al-Bukhari** are Islam's most highly respected compilers of hadeeth.

[7] www.nmm.ac.uk/server/show/conMediaFile.3139

WANT TO READ MORE?
MAY I SUGGEST?

Al-Hilali, Muhammad T. & Khan, Muhammad M., THE NOBLE Qur'an, 1996, Darussalam, Saudi Arabia, ISBN: 9960-740-79-X

American Bible Society, HOLY BIBLE (The African American Jubilee Edition)**,** Contemporary English Version, ISBN: 1-58516-020-0

Armstrong, Karen, ISLAM - A SHORT HISTORY, 2000, Random House, New York, ISBN: 0-679-64040

Asad, Muhammad. THE MESSAGE OF THE Qur'an**,** 1980, Dar Al-Andalus, Gibraltar.

Badawi, Jamal, GENDER EQUITY IN ISLAM, 1999, American Trust Publications, Indiana, ISBN: 0-89259-159-5

Green, Joey (ed.), JESUS & MUHAMMAD: The Parallel Sayings, 2003, Ulysses Press, ISBN: I-56975-326-I

Holland, Muhtar, THE DUTIES OF BROTHERHOOD IN ISLAM, 2002, The Islamic Foundation, ISBN: 0-86037-068-2

Maqsood, Ruqaiyyah Waris, WHAT EVERY CHRISTIAN SHOULD KNOW ABOUT ISLAM, 2000, The Islamic Foundation, UK, ISBN: 0-86037-375-4

Muhammad, Amir N., MUSLIMS IN AMERICA, (Seven Centuries of History 1312-2000), 2001, Amana Publications, Beltsville, MD, ISBN: 0-915957-75-2

Pickthall, Mohammed M., THE MEANING OF THE GLORIOUS [Qur'an], Penguin Books, USA, ISBN: 0-451-62857-8

Schimmel, Annemarie, ISLAM - AN INTRODUCTION, 1992, State University of New York Press, Albany, NY, ISBN: 0-7914-1328-4

GLOSSARY OF TERMS

Abrahamic Religions

Judaism, Christianity and Islam.

Al-Amin

"*The Trustworthy one.*" The nickname by which Prophet Muhammad was called by his friends, long before he became "Prophet Muhammad."

Du'a

Informal prayers. May be said in any language

Hadeeth

Hadeeth is the authentic, collected, reported sayings, actions and thoughts of Prophet Muhammad (**pbuh**) [see "Qur'an" & "sunnah" below].

Hajj

One of the five pillars of Islam. It is the pilgrimage to Mecca, Saudi Arabia. Every able-bodied Muslim who can afford the trip is required to make it at least once in her/his lifetime.[see answer #15]

Hijra

"Flight." The fleeing of Prophet Muhammad (**pbuh**) and his Muslim community from Mecca to Medina, in order to avoid persecution.

Ibrahim

The Islamic version of "Abraham."

Imam

A person who leads congregational prayers. An Islamic religious leader.

Jihad

Personal struggle, or striving. [see question 23].

Kaabah

The House of ALLAH. The most sacred shrine in Islam. When Muslims perform their formal prayers (salaah), they turn in the direction of the Kaabah. [see #V of 15]

Masjid

A House of Worship for Muslims.

Qur'an

Islam's Holy Book. Qur'an was revealed over a period of 23 years.. [see answers #12 & 13]

Rabb

Generally translated as *"Lord."* When written with the definite article, "***Al***-Rabb," it is used in Qur'an to refer ***only*** to God.

Rabbi

"Teacher." A Jewish religious leader; the chief officer of a Synagogue.

Salaah

The formal prayers which all Muslims are required to make five times a day. They are said in Arabic.

Salaam

"Peace." It is the greeting which Muslims give to Muslims, and to others.

Sawm

"Fasting." Every year, Muslims are required to fast during the month of Ramadan. They fast from dawn to sunset. every day of the month.

Shahaadah

The public declaration of faith which a person makes in order to become a Muslim. The words of the declaration are repeated often by Muslims.

Shi'ahs

One of the two major groups of Muslims. The other is the Sunnis. [see below].

Sunnah

The collected, reported sayings, actions and thoughts of Prophet Muhammad (**pbuh**). The collection is also called "hadeeth."

Sunnis

One of the two major groups of Muslims in the world. They take their name from "Sunnah." [which see above].

Ulamaa

Islamic scholars.

Zakaat

Obligatory tax which all Muslims are required to pay, and which is used for charity. Zakaat is one of the five pillars of Islam. [see question 15].

ISLAMIC CAIRO
(Stalactite Vault)

ABOUT THE AUTHOR

SHAYKH IBRAHIM ABDUL-MALIK, Ed.D., Ph.D., ***Educator, Writer, Speaker, Lecturer, Educational Consultant, Human Rights Activist*** **is director of the Centre for Empowerment and Personal Growth. Dr. Ibrahim's work with individuals, couples, family units and groups is always aimed at helping his clients to access their innate resources, and thus empower themselves.**

Dr. Ibrahim is also a Certified Master Practitioner of both Neuro-Linguistic Programming (NLP) and Ericksonian Therapeutic Hypnosis, and a member of the World Health Community of NLP Practitioners.

Dr. Ibrahim was born on Christmas day, 1923, in New York City. He earned his first doctor's degree in Science and Education at Harvard University in 1971, and his second in Islamic Studies (Ecumenical Ministries) from Graduate Theological Foundation in 2007.

After completing a 25-year, multi-leveled career with the New York City Board of Education, Dr. Ibrahim served as Science Advisor for UNESCO in the Republic of Maldives, S. E. Asia, from 1979 to 1982. There he organized and was the first Head of the ***first*** **junior college in the country. The College recently celebrated its 25th anniversary.**

In addition, he was Adjunct Professor at City University of New York (The City College and Baruch College), and for ten years (1983 - 1992), taught school-aged actors on Broadway and in Television. For eight consecutive years, he taught "Theo," "Vanessa" and "Rudy" of The Cosby Show.

Shaykh Ibrahim is presently teaching (at Fairleigh Dickinson University) courses on the ***Philosophy of Religion,*** **and** ***Women's Issues in Religion.*** **Shaykh Ibrahim is an Elder of the Admiral Family Circle Islamic Community, an arm of which, the Malik Shabazz Human Rights Institute, has been sponsoring Human Rights Education programs for several**

years. Admiral Family is accredited to the United Nations as a Non-Governmental Organization (NGO), with Special Consultative Status.

Immediately following September 11, 2001, Shaykh Ibrahim served for several months as a Red Cross Chaplain, at and near ground zero, volunteering several hours a week, counseling both survivors of the event, and families who were still grieving the loss of their loved ones. Meanwhile, he wrote a widely-distributed information booklet: *ISLAM AND MUSLIMS - Twenty-five Questions and Answers*. He is presently negotiating the publication of his completed book: *PRAYER IN ISLAM - A Guide for Beginning Muslims, An Introduction for non-Muslims*.

Shaykh Dr. Ibrahim continues to write about Islam. He is widely sought after as a speaker, and continues to be very involved in interfaith/inter-religious projects and activities with Muslim and non-Muslim organizations locally and nationally.

Rest assured that
Believers (Muslims), Jews, [and] Christians . . .
Whoever believes in Allah and the last day,
And perform[s] good deeds -
Will be rewarded by their LORD.
They will have nothing to Fear,
Or to regret.

(MALIK, *Al-Baqara*, 2:62)

NOTES